WHY YOU ARE POOR

How people think and get stuck in poverty cycle

Discover the factors for your lack

Neil W. Bustos

Copyright

No part of this publication may be reproduced, distributed, or transmitted in any form or by any means, including photocopying, recording, or other electronic or mechanical methods, without the prior written permission of the publisher, except in the case of brief quotations embodied in critical reviews and certain other noncommercial uses permitted by copyright law.

Copyright © 2022 [Neil W. Bustos]. All rights reserved.

Table of Contents

INTRODUCTION
PART I: EXTERNAL FACTORS WHY ARE YOU POOR
PART II: INTERNAL FACTORS WHY YOU ARE POOR
CONCLUSION

INTRODUCTION

We live in a world where financial wealth is commonly seen as a measure of success and happiness. Millions of people around the world, however, are not capable of attaining this goal. Many of them are underprivileged and struggle to make ends meet. However, We often hear the term "you are what you make of yourself", and for many of us, this is true. But for an increasing number of individuals, being poor is not a choice, but a horrible reality.

If you've ever felt like you're caught in a cycle of poverty, you're not alone. It's estimated that over 1.4 billion people around the world live in extreme poverty, and many of those folks are stuck in a cycle of poverty that may be hard to escape.

Growing up in poverty may be very traumatic, but it's crucial to know that poverty isn't always a result of personal failure. In actuality, many folks are born into poverty and don't have the same access to resources that affluent people enjoy. From lack of education and work possibilities to institutional racism and inadequate government resources, there is a multitude of reasons that could lead to poverty and economic inequality.

At other times, poverty may also be a result of personal choices, life events such as a death in the family, bad acts such as taking on too much debt, making imprudent investments, or spending over one's means may lead to financial troubles.

No matter the cause, poverty may have long-term harmful implications on an individual's health and well-being. Lack of access to essentials such as food, shelter, and healthcare may generate physical and mental health concerns.

While poverty is a multifaceted issue, there is no one-size-fits-all approach. However, with the perfect combination of knowledge and labor, it may be minimized and individuals might accomplish financial success.

In this book, we'll analyze in detail some of the reasons why so many folks are struggling to make ends meet. We'll also examine approaches that persons in poverty could break the pattern and improve their circumstances.

PART I: EXTERNAL FACTORS WHY ARE YOU POOR

Poverty is a problem that plagues the globe and affects individuals of all ages, colors, and origins. While numerous internal elements determine why someone may be poor, some external variables affect poverty levels. These external issues include access to education, economic policies, proper healthcare, and work possibilities. Additionally, structural inequality, environmental deterioration, and lack of access to social safety nets may all lead to poverty.

The reasons why someone may be impoverished may vary tremendously; some of them are self-inflicted and others beyond control. None of the causes behind it, poverty may have catastrophic impacts on someone's life. With little money, it may be hard to obtain essentials, and it can lead to sadness, worry, and a loss of self-esteem. In this part, we will cover the numerous external causes that might lead to poverty.

1. Economic Conditions

The economic realities of society dictate why some individuals are in poverty and others are affluent. Economic instability is one of the most essential aspects to examine while attempting to understand why someone is poor.

Economic instability happens when a country's economy is in a state of flux, resulting in fluctuations in the value of money, inflation, and other economic upheavals. When economic instability arises, it may lead to increased costs and lower incomes, making it harder to make ends meet. This is particularly true for individuals living in poverty, who frequently lack the means and assistance to withstand the storm.

Economic factors have a crucial part in deciding whether someone is poor. A person's economic condition is frequently influenced by the degree of money they make, the amount of debt they have, and their capacity to access resources to satisfy their fundamental necessities.

When the economic circumstances are weak, it might lead to increased unemployment rates and lower pay. This implies that it is difficult for individuals to get work and the earnings they receive are not adequate to satisfy their basic requirements. This may lead to poverty since individuals do not have enough money to pay for food, housing, and other requirements.

Inflation is another issue that may contribute to poverty. Inflation is a prolonged increase in the prices of goods and services. This implies that consumers have to pay more for the same things, and over time, their salaries may not be able to keep up with the growing costs. This may leave individuals with less money to cover their fundamental necessities, such as food and shelter, and can lead to poverty.

Debt may also lead to poverty. People with significant amounts of debt often find it difficult to make ends meet, since they are spending a big part of their income on paying off loans. This may lead to a cycle of debt and poverty since they are unable to save or invest in assets that might help them break out of poverty.

A lack of economic development may also contribute to poverty. Economic growth refers to a rise in the production of products and services. When economic growth is poor, it might result in less employment and lower earnings. This may hinder individuals from earning enough money to fulfill their fundamental requirements, resulting in poverty.

Finally, inequality may also lead to poverty. Inequality occurs when some individuals have more money and resources than others. This might imply that some individuals have access to greater education and career prospects, while others are left behind. This may lead to poverty for people who do not have access to the same resources as their richer peers.

In conclusion, economic situations may play a key part in deciding why some individuals are impoverished while others are affluent. Poor economic circumstances, such as high unemployment, inflation, and a lack of economic development, may contribute to poverty, while inequality can prohibit certain individuals from having the same access to resources as their richer counterparts. To eliminate poverty, it is vital to guarantee that economic circumstances are healthy and that inequality is reduced.

2. Political Environment

The political context may play a crucial influence in deciding why an individual or group of people are impoverished. This is because politics may alter the economic environment and access to resources, which are both major variables in poverty.

Political actions may have a direct influence on poverty levels. For example, a government that adopts measures that minimize poverty may be credited for lowering poverty levels in the nation. On the other hand, a government that adopts policies that exacerbate poverty may be blamed for the growth in poverty.

In addition to legislation, the political climate may also impact the economic environment. This may be via taxation laws, which can favor some firms over others, or by subsidies, which can give certain enterprises an edge over others. These policies may create an uneven economic environment, making it difficult for certain individuals to attain economic stability.

Similarly, government expenditure has a direct influence on levels of poverty. If the government concentrates its expenditure on infrastructure and investment, it may generate employment and boost economic development, which can assist in eliminating poverty. However, if the government commits more funding to the military and other non-essential expenditures, this may have a severe influence on poverty levels.

The political context may also influence access to resources. This may be done via policies that favor some groups or persons over others. For example, a government may enact laws that grant preferential access to resources, such as land and credit, to specific groups or people. This may create an uneven playing field, restricting access to resources for some and enhancing it for others.

Lastly, the political climate may influence social policy. This may be via laws that restrict or encourage access to health care, education, and other social services. These policies may have a crucial impact on poverty levels since they can decide how much access individuals have to resources that can help them overcome poverty.

In conclusion, the political environment may play a major influence in deciding whether an individual or group of people are impoverished. Policies may impact the economic environment, access to resources, and social policies, all of which can determine an individual's or group's capacity to overcome poverty. Therefore, it is vital to examine the political climate while looking at poverty levels.

3. Social Trends

Social patterns have a huge effect on why a person may be impoverished. A range of social variables, such as education level, access to economic possibilities, and employment availability, might play a role in a person's capacity to attain financial stability.

Education is a crucial aspect that impacts why someone may be impoverished. Education provides access to higher-paying occupations and economic prospects, while people with lesser levels of education are likely to encounter economic disadvantages. Additionally, persons with lesser levels of education are more likely to pick occupations with lower earnings, which makes it tougher to save money and develop wealth.

The tendency of globalization has had a profound influence on poverty. Globalization has enhanced the movement of capital and products, which has led to the greater exploitation of workers and resources, especially in poor countries. This has led to growing poverty in many nations, while salaries remain low and the cost of living is high. Additionally, the concentration of wealth in the hands of the few has led to a growth in income inequality, with the rich growing wealthier while the poor becoming poorer.

The growth of technology is another aspect that has influenced poverty. Technology has transformed the way people work, with more professions being mechanized and needing complicated expertise. This has contributed to the rising gap between the haves and the have-nots, as those with the requisite skills and knowledge enjoy the advantages while others who do not have access to technology or essential abilities are left behind.

The development of urbanization has been another key influence in the growth of poverty. Urbanization has increased the concentration of people in cities, resulting in overpopulation, insufficient housing, and poor access to essential services. This has led to a rise in poverty, as metropolitan regions become more stretched and unable to care for their residents.

Social movements and civil turmoil have also influenced poverty. Social movements such as the civil rights movement, the women's rights movement, and the LGBT rights movement have all contributed to increasing awareness of the concerns of poverty and economic inequality. These movements have increased awareness of the imbalance of resources and opportunities available to various communities and have placed pressure on governments to address these concerns.

Access to economic possibilities is another major aspect of why someone may be impoverished. Those with fewer economic prospects are more likely to be locked in low-paying employment and unable to access higher-paying careers or investments. Additionally, persons with restricted access to economic possibilities are less likely to obtain essential help, such as financial aid or grants, which makes it more difficult to get ahead financially.

Job availability may impact why someone may be poor. Many individuals find it difficult to obtain work that offers a livable wage, which makes it tough to move out of poverty. Additionally, individuals who can locate work may discover that their hours or income are not adequate to fulfill basic requirements. This might lead to financial instability and make it harder to save money or invest in the future.

Finally, socioeconomic issues such as the cost of living might also determine why someone may be poor. People living in places with higher expenses of living are likely to have more difficulties affording basic requirements, such as food and accommodation. Additionally, persons residing in places with high expenses of living may be unable to access higher-paying employment or services, making it harder to go ahead financially.

Ultimately, societal patterns have a huge effect on why someone may be poor. Education, access to economic prospects, employment availability, and the cost of living may all influence a person's capacity to reach financial stability. Globalization, technology, urbanization, and social movements have also all led to a rise in poverty and inequality. Without addressing these concerns, poverty will continue to be a big problem in both developed and developing nations but by understanding how it may impact poverty, people and communities can work together to build a more fair and prosperous society.

4. Natural Calamities

The influence of natural catastrophes on poverty levels is frequently neglected but may be far-reaching and long-lasting. Natural catastrophes such as floods, hurricanes, and earthquakes may have a severe impact on a nation's economy, leading to increased levels of poverty.

Natural catastrophes may ruin homes, disrupt livelihoods, and wipe away funds, leaving people with no means to obtain basic requirements such as food, water, and shelter. The damage to infrastructure also inhibits people from accessing services like healthcare, education, and work opportunities, further entrenching them in poverty.

Natural disasters may also inflict substantial damage to agriculture, resulting in food shortages and hunger. Crop losses may cause a rise in food costs, which might be prohibitive for individuals in poverty. Furthermore, the loss of agricultural land may substantially diminish the earnings of farmers, leading to a rise in poverty.

Natural catastrophes may also contribute to a spike in unemployment if individuals are unable to obtain jobs or locate new ones. This may further increase poverty levels since individuals are unable to earn enough money to satisfy their fundamental requirements.

When natural catastrophes hit, it may be expensive to repair or restore the damage, and the expenses are frequently shared by the government or the public. In underdeveloped nations, where resources are already tight, the expense of repairs may be a tremendous burden on the economy. As a consequence, government money is diverted away from other sectors such as health, education, and other social initiatives, to pay for disaster assistance. This leads to limited access to fundamental services such as healthcare and education, resulting in a loss in quality of life and a rise in poverty levels.

In addition, natural calamities may contribute to the relocation of people. People may be compelled to abandon their homes, employment, and communities and seek sanctuary in other locations. This displacement may be a significant cause of poverty, since individuals may not have the wherewithal to start over in a new region. It may also lead to a disruption of conventional livelihoods, since individuals may not be able to continue their employment owing to the destruction of their workplace or the lack of resources in a new area.

Finally, natural catastrophes may create an interruption in services and commodities, resulting in a rise in the costs of goods and services. This may have a particularly severe impact on individuals in poverty since they cannot afford to pay increased costs. have a catastrophic influence on poverty levels. It is consequently vital to invest in disaster risk reduction methods to help alleviate the consequences of natural catastrophes on poverty.

5. Racism and Social Exclusion

Racism and social exclusion have a major influence on why people are poor. Racism has been used as a tactic to oppress and marginalize whole groups of people, making them more likely to be impoverished. African Americans, for example, have endured institutional racism since the days of slavery, which still undermines their economic chances and resources now. This racism has been a key factor in the income difference between African Americans and White Americans.

Social exclusion may also have a substantial influence on why individuals are poor. Social exclusion is being excluded from particular social groups and networks. This may lead to individuals feeling ostracized, alone, and detached from mainstream society, making it harder to access the resources and opportunities required to attain economic stability. People who are socially excluded may not have the same access to education and career possibilities as those who are included. This may lead to a lack of economic stability and poverty.

When individuals endure racism and social exclusion, they confront a lack of opportunity and resources that may otherwise be utilized to better their financial status. This may lead to individuals being unable to obtain jobs, education, or housing, all of which can contribute to poverty. Furthermore, racism and social exclusion may contribute to individuals being hesitant to engage in the economic system, since they may feel unwanted or unjustly assessed. This may produce a feeling of pessimism and despair, which can lead to individuals avoiding any form of financial engagement.

Racism and social exclusion may also have a psychological effect on individuals. People who suffer racism and social exclusion may feel alone, inferior, and disempowered, leading to feelings of sadness and anxiety. This might lead to individuals avoiding activities and chances that they could utilize to enhance their financial status.

Racism and social exclusion may also contribute to individuals feeling marginalized and helpless. This may make individuals more willing to take risks that may further worsen their poverty, such as taking out high-interest loans or participating in criminal activities. The lack of access to resources and opportunities, along with feelings of helplessness may further entrench individuals in poverty.

In conclusion, racism and social exclusion may have a substantial influence on why individuals are poor. Systemic racism has been a key factor in the income difference between African Americans and White Americans. Social exclusion may make it harder for individuals to access the resources and opportunities required to attain economic stability. Finally, emotions of marginalization and helplessness may lead to individuals taking risks that might entrench them in poverty.

6. Failing Health

Failing health may have a dramatic influence on why someone is impoverished. Poor health may lead to an incapacity to work or may cause a person to not be able to work as many hours or at a job that pays them enough to make ends meet. Poor health may also cause medical expenditures to mount up, leaving a person unable to pay for their fundamental requirements.

Poor health might make it difficult for someone to engage in the workforce. Chronic diseases, impairments, or other health difficulties might make it difficult or impossible to work full-time, or at a job that pays enough to meet necessities. Additionally, bad health might prohibit someone from being able to get a job in the first place. For example, a person with a chronic disease may not be able to find work that is flexible enough to satisfy their health demands.

Poor health might also contribute to excessive medical expenditures. Medical costs may mount up rapidly, even for individuals with health insurance. For people without health insurance, the expenditures might be substantially greater. Additionally, medical fees might prohibit someone from being able to prepare for the future or pay for other required obligations.

Finally, bad health may lead to emotional and mental discomfort, which can have a major influence on someone's capacity to work and make ends meet. People with poor health frequently have to struggle with sadness, anxiety, and other mental health difficulties. These challenges might make it difficult for someone to concentrate on their job or to get out of bed and go to work each day.

In summary, declining health may have a substantial influence on why someone is poor. Poor health may prohibit someone from being able to work, can lead to expensive medical expenditures, and can create emotional and mental pain. All of these may make it difficult for someone to make ends meet, and can contribute to a person's poverty.

7. Death

Death may have a huge influence on why someone may be impoverished. It might be caused to the death of a key earner in a family, or the incapacity of a surviving family member to take over the function of the dead. In certain situations, the loss of a loved one may create a huge emotional and financial hardship, leading to destitution.

When a major earner dies, the family may not be able to replace that income or support. This may lead to poverty since the surviving family members are unable to make ends meet. In other circumstances, there may be no support structure in place to assist with the extra expenditures linked with the death, such as funeral fees, hospital bills, and other obligations. This might put the family in a terrible financial condition, since they may not have the means to fend for themselves.

The loss of a loved one may also create emotional and psychological stress, which can lead to poverty. The death of a family member may induce sadness, melancholy, and worry, which can make it difficult for someone to obtain and retain a job. This might lead to a drop in income and induce poverty.

The loss of a loved one may also create a social disturbance, since the family may have to migrate to another place to find employment or start a new life. This might lead to a lack of access to resources and social networks, which can be a hurdle to getting a job and being financially secure.

Finally, death may generate poverty if the dead leaves behind debts or other responsibilities that the remaining family members are accountable for. This might make it tough to manage their money and can lead to poverty.

In conclusion, death may have a dramatic influence on why someone may be impoverished. The loss of a major earner, emotional and psychological stress, social disturbance, and financial burdens may all contribute to poverty. It is crucial to be aware of these possible implications of death and to be prepared to assist those impacted.

PART II: INTERNAL FACTORS WHY YOU ARE POOR

Being poor is a challenging condition to be in. It may be a consequence of many various circumstances, both external and internal. Internal variables are those that are under our control, such as our attitude, beliefs, decision-making, and conduct. Our internal variables form the basis of how we conduct our lives and maybe huge impacts on our success or failure.

Another essential internal aspect is our thinking. Our mentality is our attitude and ideas about ourselves and the world around us. It may influence our capacity to attain our objectives and to endure when presented with adversity. If our mind is positive, we are more likely to succeed because we are more willing to take risks and be enthusiastic about our possibilities of success. However, if our thinking is negative, we may feel disheartened and quit quickly.

It is crucial to understand these internal reasons that are impacting our poverty to generate answers and make progress to move away from poverty toward a better financial future. This section will address some of the internal elements that might lead to poverty.

1. Financial Illiteracy

Financial illiteracy is one of the key reasons why many people are impoverished. Financial illiteracy is characterized as the absence of information, skills, and comprehension of fundamental financial concepts, such as budgeting, saving, investing, and debt management. This lack of understanding leads to poor decision-making, which in turn leads to poverty.

Financial illiteracy may lead to the incapacity to make good financial choices. For example, those with insufficient financial understanding may be unable to look forward and prepare for their future. This might lead to choices that put them in debt or lead to overspending. Poor financial choices may lead to a cycle of debt that gets progressively difficult to break out of.

Financially illiterate people may also be unable to spot attractive investment possibilities. They may not comprehend how to diversify their money or how to compare various options. Without the information to pick the appropriate investments, people may wind up losing money instead of expanding their fortune.

Another consequence of financial illiteracy is the inability to obtain financial goods and services. Without a basic grasp of financial goods and services, consumers may not be able to obtain the resources they need to better their financial status. This may further worsen financial troubles and lead to an even deeper cycle of poverty.

Finally, financial illiteracy is a big element in why individuals are impoverished. People who are unfamiliar with the fundamentals of financial problems are more prone to make bad financial judgments. This may lead to a cycle of debt and financial instability that can be difficult to break out of. Financial literacy is a crucial skill to acquire to break out of poverty and obtain financial stability.

2. Wrong Mindset About Money

Money is one of the most powerful forces in the world and it is commonly understood that possessing a certain amount of money may provide a certain degree of comfort and security to one's life. Unfortunately, many individuals have a faulty perspective when it comes to money and this may be a key contributing cause to why they stay poor.

Most individuals who are impoverished have a scarcity perspective regarding money. This implies that they feel there is not enough money to go around, therefore they hoard whatever they have and never take chances in investing or developing their fortune. This thinking leads to a sense of powerlessness and helplessness, which may keep individuals locked in poverty.

The most prevalent erroneous thinking regarding money is the notion that it would fix all of our issues. They assume that money would cure all their issues and enable them to acquire everything they desire. This is a terrible trap to slip into since it may lead to irresponsible spending and unwise judgments. It's vital to remember that money is merely a tool and it cannot substitute hard work and devotion. Having a good relationship with money is vital for anybody who wants to be successful.

Other impoverished individuals have a bad attitude toward money. They may consider money as the foundation of all evil or something that only corrupt people utilize. This mentality drives people to shy away from money, which hinders them from taking advantage of financial possibilities that may help them move out of poverty.

Another incorrect perspective regarding money is the assumption that it can purchase happiness. While it's true that money may purchase some comforts, it cannot buy real and lasting happiness. People who adopt this sort of thinking may find themselves always running after more and more money, never feeling happy.

Finally, another erroneous perspective regarding money is the assumption that it is the only way to be successful. This is also a hazardous trap since it may drive individuals to disregard other vital elements of their life such as their physical health, spiritual welfare, and relationships. Having a balanced attitude to life is vital to be successful.

Having an incorrect perspective about money might be a big contributing element to why someone stays poor. It is crucial to have a healthy attitude towards money and to recognize that it is merely a tool, not an end-all answer. The key to overcoming poverty is to have a good attitude and thinking regarding money. Start by defining realistic financial objectives and preparing a budget to help you remain on track. Find strategies to enhance your income, such as taking a second job or establishing a company. Invest your money in areas that will build your wealth, such as equities, real estate, and mutual funds. Finally, money should not be the only thing that motivates you, but rather something that helps you reach your objectives and aspirations.

3. Entitlement Mentality

In today's environment, there is an ever-increasing number of individuals who have formed an entitlement mindset. An entitlement attitude is something that many individuals suffer from, and it may have a devastating influence on an individual's financial welfare. An entitlement attitude is when a person believes they deserve certain things without having to put in the effort to achieve them. This might lead to an 'it's all about me' mentality when the person fails to understand their role in accomplishing their objectives. It may also lead to emotions of victimhood, low self-esteem, and a lack of drive which can have a major influence on why you are poor.

The entitlement mindset is founded in a feeling of entitlement, or the conviction that one deserves something merely because of their identity or position. This idea may cause people to behave in ways that are not in their best interest and can restrict their capacity for development and achievement. This might lead to a person not accepting responsibility for their own money. They may assume that they are entitled to money or belongings that they have not worked for or earned, and this may lead to a lack of financial planning and budgeting. Without taking the time to organize their money, the person may find themselves in a position where they are not able to pay their obligations or save for the future, resulting in financial difficulty.

Entitled persons may become arrogant and demanding, expecting others to do things for them without any work on their side. This may generate a climate of animosity, as others around the entitled person will frequently feel taken advantage of and undervalued. This, in turn, may lead to strained relationships, since people who are feeling taken advantage of will frequently be less eager to support the entitled person in the future.

It may also lead to an unrealistic picture of life. The person may anticipate attaining their objectives without putting in the required hard effort and devotion. This may lead to emotions of disappointment when their expectations are not realized, and this can lead to a sense of despair.

To avoid slipping into the trap of entitlement attitude, it is necessary to realize your responsibilities when it comes to accomplishing your financial objectives.

It is also crucial to establish reasonable objectives and expectations and to be prepared to put in the work to accomplish them. Taking the effort to budget and plan your money will enable you to remain on track and attain your financial objectives.

Being aware of the hazards of an entitlement attitude will assist you to avoid sliding into a position where you are impoverished. Understanding your involvement in reaching your financial objectives and taking the required efforts to accomplish them will enable you to have a secure financial future.

Finally, the entitlement attitude may contribute to a sense of poverty. Those who feel that they are entitled to anything without any effort on their side will frequently not take the initiative to enhance their abilities, network, or discover better career prospects. As a consequence, individuals may be locked in low-paying employment and never be able to break out of poverty.

4. Laziness

Laziness is a quality that frequently has a bad connotation, yet it may have a big influence on one's financial condition. There are indeed numerous external reasons that might lead to poverty, but it's fair to state that idleness is a big role in many situations.

Laziness is a big element in why many individuals are poor. If you are lazy, you are more likely to be locked in a cycle of poverty. This is because lazy individuals typically lack the drive and ambition to work hard, gain new skills, and enhance their life. When someone is lazy, they are less likely to make the effort to locate a better job, seek an education, or save money.

Lazy individuals are more inclined to settle for minimal-pay occupations that provide limited opportunities for upward mobility. They may be less motivated to hunt for higher-paid positions, take on occupations with no benefits such as those in the gig economy, or create their enterprises. They may also be more inclined to submit to peer pressure and make unwise financial choices which leave them exposed to financial instability.

When it comes to making money, certain procedures need to be performed to assure success. These phases involve establishing objectives, budgeting, planning, and taking regular action. If someone is lazy, they are less likely to follow these actions and as a consequence, their income will decrease.

Laziness might also prohibit someone from taking advantage of educational and financial opportunities. For example, if someone is too lazy to investigate scholarships or apply for grants, they may lose out on the possibility to go to college or obtain financial help. Even if someone has the financial resources to attend school, they may not have the motivation or drive to push themselves to achieve and make the most of their education.

The same applies to investment. Such who are lazy may not take the time to investigate the finest assets and they may not have the discipline to remain with those investments over the long run. As a consequence, they may wind up losing money.

In conclusion, laziness may be a primary factor in why someone is poor. If someone is lazy, they are less likely to take advantage of financial and educational opportunities, make sensible financial judgments, and manage their assets properly. All of this may lead to poverty in the long term.

5. Excuses

From infancy, we are taught that excuses are a negative thing—they are a show of weakness and a lack of responsibility. But when it comes to poverty, People frequently create excuses to avoid accepting responsibility for their actions and decisions. It is also a technique to escape the hard effort and devotion it takes to attain financial success.

When someone is poor, their living circumstances may sometimes lead to a broad variety of justifications. For example, they may lack the appropriate knowledge or skills to acquire a career that pays well, or they may have suffered from a health crisis or family tragedy that has emptied their resources. Other justifications can include living in a low socio-economic location or being discriminated against due to race or gender.

The most frequent excuse individuals make when it comes to money is that they don't have enough of it. This argument is commonly used to rationalize why people can't purchase the goods they desire or why they can't save money. Yet, this explanation entirely overlooks the reality that it's feasible to produce more money via hard effort, devotion, and wise financial choices.

Another typical reason is that individuals don't have enough time to concentrate on reaching financial success. This argument generally arises from the perception that producing more money involves too much work and that it's better to just remain in the same financial situation. However, this justification is incorrect because it overlooks the reality that there are various alternatives to produce money outside of typical work.

From beginning a side company to investing in stocks, there are numerous possibilities open to those who are prepared to put in the work.

These excuses can influence why someone is poor because they give a clearer explanation of the circumstances that have led to their poverty. It can be easier to understand why someone is poor when their reasons are laid out in detail.

Finally, another excuse people often make is that they don't have enough knowledge or skills to be financially successful. This excuse is rooted in fear and insecurity, and it prevents people from learning the skills they need to increase their financial stability.

The truth is, excuses are a major contributor to poverty. People who make excuses are more likely to continue in the same financial situation, whereas those who accept responsibility and make adjustments are more likely to attain financial success. Therefore, if you want to be financially successful, it's necessary to accept responsibility for your actions and quit making excuses. With commitment and hard effort, you may attain the financial success that you seek.

6. Unhealthy Lifestyle Habits

Poverty is one of the most important concerns confronting the globe today, with more than 1 billion people living in severe poverty. While numerous variables lead to poverty, unhealthy behaviors may also play a role. These behaviors may vary from addiction to poor judgment, etc, and can have a huge influence on an individual's life. Not only can these behaviors create severe financial hardship, but they may also hinder a person from learning critical skills for economic success. We will cover some of these tendencies in this section.

a. Ignoring Education and Training Opportunities

When it comes to a person's financial success, education and training opportunities may play a key influence. By disregarding educational and training opportunities, people are placing themselves in danger of financial difficulty. Education and training are vital factors in learning information, developing skills, and gaining useful experience that will enable you to become successful and rich.

Educational opportunities offer a person with the information and abilities to excel in the profession. Without this knowledge and skill set, someone is more likely to struggle to get a job, much alone a well-paying one and without a job, you are more likely to suffer poverty.

Training is also a key aspect of success. Training supplies us with the practical skills required to execute a job efficiently. It can educate us on how to utilize various tools and technology, as well as how to communicate with people. These courses and programs provide people the ability to study and perhaps achieve new certifications that may help them find a job or climb up the corporate ladder. Without these opportunities, people may struggle to perform at their best and may not be able to obtain the job they desire, additionally disregarding these opportunities is to restrict your capacity to become successful.

b. Poor Time Management

Poor time management may have a huge influence on why you are poor. When you don't manage your time effectively, it may lead to lost opportunities, wasted time, and an overall lack of productivity. This may have a major influence on your capacity to generate money and attain financial success.

When you don't manage your time well, you may lose out on critical opportunities that may help you generate more money. For example, you may miss deadlines for applying for jobs or promotions, or you may miss out on networking events that might lead to professional improvements. Additionally, if you don't manage your time well, you may wind yourself squandering time on things that don't add to your financial success. This might involve browsing through social media, watching television, or indulging in other things that don't help you create more money or develop your career.

Poor time management may also contribute to a lack of productivity. When you don't manage your time efficiently, you may find yourself delaying or difficult to concentrate on the activities that you need to do. This may lead to missed deadlines, incomplete tasks, and an overall lack of development. This may prohibit you from obtaining success in your profession, as well as hamper your potential to produce more money.

Additionally, poor time management may contribute to a lack of motivation and a sensation of being overburdened. When you don't manage your time appropriately, it may be tough to remain motivated and on track with your objectives. This might lead to a sensation of being overwhelmed and feeling that you can't do anything. This might make it tough to concentrate on producing more money and attaining financial success.

Summary: Poor time management may lead to a lack of concentration and efficiency, both of which can be key contributors to financial instability. Without a strategy or framework, activities may take longer than intended, resulting in missed deadlines and lost opportunities. Additionally, poor time management may lead to poor decision-making, which can lead to expensive blunders and poor investments. Without a suitable strategy and timeframe, it may be difficult to prioritize work, resulting in a loss of productivity and perhaps, a lack of money. Poor time management may also lead to instances of procrastination, which can further impair financial security.

c. Living Beyond Your Means

When it comes to financial success, living within your means is a critical component. Unfortunately, many individuals fall into the trap of living beyond their means and end up in a cycle of poverty. Here are a few ways living over your means might impact why you are poor.

The most apparent way living beyond your means impacts your financial health is by generating a cycle of debt. When you spend more money than you have, you need to borrow cash to offset the deficit. This leads to interest payments, late fines, and other expenses that may mount up rapidly. The more debt you have, the harder it is to pay it off and the more interest you will have to pay. This might establish a cycle of debt that can be hard to stop.

Another way living beyond your means might harm your financial health is that it can hinder you from establishing an emergency fund or investing for retirement. When you are living paycheck to paycheck, it might be tough to save away any money for the future. This might leave you with no financial buffer in the case of an emergency or retirement, placing you in an extremely hazardous financial position.

Finally, living beyond your means might have a toll on your mental health. The stress and worry that come from continuously striving to keep up with the Joneses may take a toll on your mental health. This might lead to sadness, anxiety, and other mental health disorders that can further influence your financial circumstances.

Summary: Living beyond your means is a highly harmful habit that may have a lasting influence on your financial health. It may lead to a cycle of debt, impede you from saving for the future, and have a detrimental influence on your mental health. If you find yourself living beyond your means, it's crucial to take measures to get back on track and start living within your means.

d. Addiction

Addiction is a big element in why many people are impoverished. Whether it's alcohol, drugs, or gambling, addiction can have a terrible influence on an individual's finances. Not only can an addiction cause a person to lose money in the near term, but it may also have long-term implications that make it impossible for them to ever move out of poverty.

One of the most immediate repercussions of addiction is an individual's inability to keep down a job. Addiction creates cognitive deficits that might make it difficult to concentrate on activities or remain motivated. This may lead to poor work performance, which can lead to a person being fired or laid off. Even if a person can hold a job, their addiction may force them to take days off or come in late, both of which may diminish their income or lead to disciplinary action.

Addiction often generates additional financial concerns. For example, someone may spend a considerable part of their money on drugs or activities to which they are addicted. This might leave them without enough money to pay for essentials such as food, clothes, and rent. An addiction may also motivate a person to engage in unlawful acts to sustain their habit, resulting in court bills or penalties that further deplete their income.

Finally, addiction may lead to a person losing essential connections, such as family or friends. This might lead individuals to be isolated, making it harder to locate assistance or resources to help them better their financial circumstances. A person may also lose vital relationships that may have helped them find a job or accommodation.

Summary: Addiction may have a terrible impact on an individual's finances. It may lead them to lose their career, spend too much money on their addiction, and ruin crucial relationships. These financial concerns might make it impossible for a person to ever overcome poverty. If you or someone you know is battling with addiction, it is crucial to get assistance as soon as possible to avoid long-term financial ramifications.

e. Investing In Get Rich Quick Schemes

Investing in get-rich-quick schemes is generally considered a certain method to generate money fast and effortlessly. However, this form of investment may be a deadly trap that might leave you poorer than when you began.

When it comes to get-rich-quick schemes, the promises of rapid and easy money sometimes appear too good to be true. These schemes often entail investing with the hope of a big return in a short period. However, the fact is that these strategies generally end in losses instead of gains.

The reason for this is that these schemes are generally founded on misleading promises, unreasonable assumptions, and fraudulent acts. They depend on people's desire to earn a lot of money with no work, and they may easily abuse those who are inexperienced in the financial environment.

The risk of investing in get-rich-quick schemes is that you might lose all of your money in a matter of days or weeks. If the strategy includes investing in a risky item or involves illegal activity, you might even wind yourself facing legal action.

In addition, you might wind up paying exorbitant charges for investing in get-rich-quick schemes. This might further erode your earnings and leave you with less money than you began with.

Finally, investment in get-rich-quick schemes might lead to a false feeling of security. You may feel that you have discovered a certain approach to making money, and this may lead to overconfidence and incorrect actions. This might lead to further losses and ultimately put you in an even worse financial condition.

Summary: Investing in get-rich-quick programs may be a risky trap that might leave you less than when you began. It's vital to be aware of the hazards involved and to be sure to conduct your homework before making any investments. By adopting a more careful approach, you may guarantee that your money is invested more safely and sustainably.

CONCLUSION

Poverty is a big problem that affects individuals of all ages and origins. It has a tremendous influence on the quality of life of people, families, and communities. Poverty may lead to a range of negative repercussions, including poor health, low educational achievement, and lower economic stability.

At an individual level, poverty may have a terrible influence on someone's life. People who are living in poverty generally struggle to make ends meet and may experience food insecurity, restricted access to healthcare, and insufficient housing. These difficulties may lead to physical, emotional, and mental health concerns. Furthermore, poverty may restrict educational possibilities, making it harder for people to learn the skills and information essential for future employment and upward social mobility.

At the household and societal level, poverty may have a ripple effect. Children from low-income households may have trouble obtaining appropriate educational opportunities, making it harder for them to break the cycle of poverty. Communities may also be impacted by poverty since it can lead to greater crime rates, social instability, and economic stagnation.

Although poverty is a serious concern in today's culture, it doesn't have to be a life sentence. With the correct mentality and resources, anybody can break out of poverty and attain financial independence. Here are some pointers to help you get started:

1. Take use of available resources. Many government programs, charities, and other groups give financial support to persons in need. Do your homework and find out what's available in your region.

2. Build a budget and stick to it. Having a budget can allow you to keep track of your costs and make sure you're living within your means. It will also help you save for your future.

3. Make education a priority. Education is a crucial component of success. Invest in yourself by taking advantage of educational possibilities. Whether it's via a local community college or online programs, these tools may help you build the skills you need to succeed.

4. Develop a plan. Write out your objectives and establish a strategy on how to attain them. Having a roadmap can assist keep you on track and inspired.

5. Look for employment opportunities. Look for jobs in your area or look into starting your own business. Being able to sustain oneself financially is a crucial aspect of breaking out of poverty.

6. Make contacts. Networking is crucial in every job. Attend events and create relationships with individuals who may support you in your path.

Breaking out of poverty may be a lengthy and arduous path. It involves hard effort, devotion, and drive. However, with the correct resources and mentality, it is possible to break out of poverty and attain financial independence.

Printed in Great Britain
by Amazon